MW01064293

History for Kids: The Illustrated Lives of Julius Caesar & Cleopatra

By Charles River Editors

Bronze Statue of Caesar in Rimini, Italy

About Charles River Editors

Charles River Editors was founded by Harvard and MIT alumni to provide superior editing and original writing services, with the expertise to create digital content for publishers across a vast range of subject matter. In addition to providing original digital content for third party publishers, Charles River Editors republishes civilization's greatest literary works, bringing them to a new generation via ebooks.

Introduction

Flowers left at Caesar's grave, a tradition which still continues more than 2,000 years after his death.

Julius Caesar (100-44 B.C.)

"I would rather be the first man in a humble village, than the second man in Rome" – Caesar

In Charles River Editors' History for Kids series, your children can learn about history's most important people and events in an easy, entertaining, and educational way. Pictures help bring the story to life, and the concise but comprehensive book will keep your kid's attention all the way to the end.

Possibly the most important man of antiquity, and even all of history, was Julius Caesar. Alexander Hamilton, the famous American patriot, once remarked that "the greatest man who ever lived was Julius Caesar". Such a tribute, coming from one of the Founding Fathers of the quintessential modern democracy in reference to a man who destroyed the Roman Republic, is testament to the enduring mark that Caesar left upon the world. The ultimate conqueror, statesman, dictator, visionary, and opportunist, during his time in power Caesar expanded the borders of Rome to almost twice their previous size, revolutionized the infrastructure of the Roman state, and destroyed the Roman Republic for good, leaving a line of emperors in its place.

His legacy is so strong that his name has become, in many languages, synonymous with power: the Emperors of Austria and Germany bore the title *Kaiser*, and the *Czars* of Russia also owe the etymology of their title to Caesar. His name also crept further eastward out of Europe, even cropping up in Hindi and Urdu, where the term for "Emperor" is *Kaiser.*

Even in his time, Caesar was in many ways larger than life, and because of his legacy as virtual founder of the Roman Empire, much of what was written about – and by – him during his life and immediately after his assassination was politically motivated. His successor, Octavian Augustus, had a strong interest in ensuring that Caesar's life be painted in a favorable light, while Caesar's political enemies attempted to paint him as a corrupt, undemocratic dictator who was destroying the old order of the Republic. This makes it exceedingly difficult to separate historical fact from apocryphal interjection, as the writings of Cicero (a rival of Caesar's) and the later biographies of Suetonius and Plutarch can be misleading. Nonetheless, along with Caesar's *De Bello Gallico*, his famous notes on his campaign against the Gauls, they remain our chief sources for Caesar's life – a life everyone agreed was nothing short of remarkable and changed the course of history forever.

History for Kids: The Illustrated Lives of Julius Caesar and Cleopatra provides an entertaining look at the facts and myths surrounding Rome's most famous leader and explains his legacy, which has only grown larger over 2,000 years and promises to last many more. Along with pictures of important people, places, and events, your kids will learn about Caesar like never before.

Depiction of Cleopatra and Caesarion

Cleopatra (69-30 B.C.)

"Her beauty, as we are told, was in itself not altogether incomparable, nor such as to strike those who saw her; but converse with her had an irresistible charm, and her presence, combined with the persuasiveness of her discourse and the character which was somehow diffused about her behaviour towards others, had something stimulating about it. There was sweetness also in the tones of her voice; and her tongue, like an instrument of many strings, she could readily turn to whatever language she pleased..." – Plutarch

In Charles River Editors' History for Kids series, your children can learn about history's most important people and events in an easy, entertaining, and educational way. Pictures help bring the story to life, and the concise but comprehensive book will keep your kid's attention all the way to the end.

During one of the most turbulent periods in the history of Rome, men like Julius Caesar, Mark Antony, and Octavian participated in two civil wars that would spell the end of the Roman Republic and determine who would become the Roman emperor. In the middle of it all was history's most famous woman, the Egyptian pharaoh Cleopatra (69-30 B.C.), who famously seduced both Caesar and Antony and thereby positioned herself as one of the most influential people in a world of powerful men.

Cleopatra was a legendary figure even to contemporary Romans and the ancient world, as

Plutarch's quote suggests, and she was a controversial figure who was equally reviled and praised through the years, depicted as a benevolent ruler and an evil seductress, sometimes at the same time. Over 2,000 years after her death, everything about Cleopatra continues to fascinate people around the world, from her lineage as a Ptolemaic pharaoh, her physical features, the manner in which she seduced Caesar, her departure during the Battle of Actium, and her famous suicide. And despite being one of the most famous figures in history, there is still much mystery surrounding her, leading historians and archaeologists scouring Alexandria, Egypt for clues about her life and the whereabouts of her royal palace and tomb.

History for Kids: The Illustrated Lives of Julius Caesar & Cleopatra chronicles the amazing life of Egypt's most famous pharaoh, explores some of the mysteries and myths surrounding her, and analyzes her legacy, which has only grown larger over 2,000 years and promises to last many more. Along with pictures of important people, places, and events, your kids will learn about Cleopatra like never before.

Chapter 1: Caesar's Early Life

"If you must break the law, do it to seize power; in all other cases observe it." - Caesar

Gaius Julius Caesar was born on July 12, 100 B.C.. He was the son of an important family. His family had lived in Rome for hundreds of years.

When Caesar was still a little boy, he began having seizures. Doctors didn't know how to treat it. People didn't know what seizures were. Caesar was afraid people would think something was wrong with him. Only his best friends knew about them.

When Julius Caesar was growing up, a lot of people were trying to rule Rome. Roman soldiers were fighting in Italy and other countries. People who had a lot of money were fighting people who had no money. Caesar's uncle, Gaius Marius, was helping people with less money. He wanted soldiers to be able to own land. Soldiers liked their leaders and would fight for them even if they had to fight against Rome. One of the soldiers was Sulla. He wanted to rule Rome by himself.

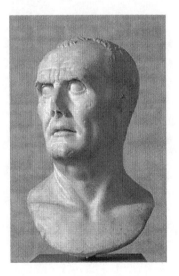

A statue of Gaius Marius

A statue of Sulla

Sulla started fighting against other Romans. The war was called Rome's first civil war. Sulla was winning. But when he left for a new battle, Marius came to Rome with an army. Marius took over Rome and got rid of Sulla's friends.

Marius died in 86 B.C. When he died, his friends got to stay in power. This was good for Julius Caesar. When he was 15, Caesar was named High Priest of Jupiter. This was a good position for a young boy. Caesar was also the head of his family. His father had died in 87 B.C.

Caesar was in love with a girl from a poor family. When his father died, it meant Caesar had to marry a woman with more money. Caesar married a young girl named Cornelia. She was the daughter of Sulla's friend Cinna. Cinna was the strongest man in Rome in 86 B.C. But then Sulla came back to Rome. Cinna's armies joined Sulla and killed Cinna in 82 B.C.

When he got back to Rome, Sulla was the only ruler of Rome. His soldiers killed Marius's friends. Caesar was in trouble because he was Marius's nephew. Sulla took his land, money and his position as High Priest of Jupiter. Caesar almost had to give up his wife too. When Sulla said he was going to kill him, Caesar had to run away and hide. His mother's family was friends with Sulla. They were able to keep Caesar from being killed.

Caesar couldn't be in Rome anymore. He joined the army. He wouldn't have been able to do this if he was still High Priest of Jupiter. But Caesar would find out that the army was good for him. He would be Rome's greatest soldier.

Chapter 2: Power

"Fortune, which has a great deal of power in other matters but especially in war, can bring about great changes in a situation through very slight forces." - Caesar

Caesar was a soldier when he joined the army. But he worked hard and was good at it. He won an award. It was called the Civic Crown.

In 80 B.C. Sulla was no longer the ruler of Rome. When Sulla was gone, Caesar felt it was safe to go to Rome again. He worked as a lawyer. He also talked a lot in Rome. He was good at arguing. He would wave his hands around and talk loudly. Caesar wanted to get better. He got on a ship to sail to Greece. He would study how to talk in public there.

Caesar never got to Greece. His ship was attacked by pirates. Caesar was taken prisoner. He was put on a small island. Caesar was calm about being a prisoner. He acted like he did not mind. He even told the pirates that he would come back for them and kill them all. The pirates thought he was making a joke. They told Caesar they were going to make his men pay 20 silver coins to get him back. Caesar said, "Twenty? Caesar is worth twice as much, and more. Ask for fifty". The pirates asked for 50 silver coins. Caesar's friends paid them. But as soon as he was free, Caesar got some boats. Then he found the pirates and killed them.

Caesar was good at leading soldiers. After he killed the pirates, he attacked the country of Pontus. He beat their army badly. When he went back to Rome in 73 B.C., Caesar was made the leader of the army.

Caesar wanted to be a politician too. Being a leader of the army helped a lot. When his wife died in 69 B.C., Caesar left Rome. He went to Spain. Rome ruled Spain at the time. Caesar was made the governor of Spain. He was a powerful Roman now.

There was another powerful man still in Rome. His name was Pompey. He was known as Pompey the Great. Caesar married Pompey's sister. This helped him get better positions in Rome. In 63 B.C., Caesar acted as a lawyer again. Cicero was also acting as a lawyer. Cicero was Rome's best speaker. But Caesar won the case. It helped Caesar become High Priest of all of Rome.

Cicero

In 62 B.C., a Roman named Catiline made a plan to take over Rome. But the plan was found out. Cicero talked in the Senate about Catiline and his plan. He made other people mad at Catiline. People who were going to help Catiline wouldn't help either. Some people thought Caesar was part of Catiline's plan. But Caesar didn't know about it. Catiline was killed in 62 B.C. But Caesar was safe.

Cesare Maccari's painting of Cicero talking about Catiline in the Roman Senate

In 60 B.C., Caesar divorced Pompey's sister. People were talking about her. They thought she may have done something wrong. Caesar wasn't sure. But he said, "Caesar's wife must be above suspicion". He didn't want people mad at him because of his wife.

In 60 B.C., Caesar didn't know what to do next. He owed a lot of money to people. He asked Crassus for help. Crassus was the richest man in Rome. He had also won a war against Spartacus. Spartacus was a gladiator who helped slaves get away from their masters. Rome loved Crassus when he beat Spartacus. Crassus helped make Caesar the governor of part of Spain.

A statue of Crassus

Caesar didn't want to pay the money he owed. He went to Spain even when he was still High Priest of All of Rome. He wanted to be governor of Spain so that he wouldn't have to pay. Roman governors could not be arrested back then.

Governors were in charge of the soldiers working in their land. This was how Caesar became the leader of an army. Caesar led the soldiers in Spain against people who were fighting the Romans there. He won two wars. This helped make him the Commander of the Roman army. The Romans liked to have a party for the Commander in Rome. It was called a triumph. It was like being king for a day.

Caesar didn't want a triumph. He wanted to be a Consul of Rome in 59 B.C. Consuls were the most powerful men in Rome. People had to be elected as consuls. They only got to be consuls for a year. A consul couldn't be in the army either. Crassus told Caesar he should try to be consul too.

In 59 B.C., Caesar won. He was now a consul. The other consul was named Marcus Bibulus. Caesar and Crassus were able to work with Pompey. This meant they wouldn't have to fight each other. By working together, Caesar, Crassus and Pompey became the three biggest leaders in Rome. They were called the First Triumvirate. Crassus had the money, Pompey had the soldiers, and Caesar had the ideas.

A statue of Pompey

Caesar did a lot of things that people didn't like when he was consul. He knew he would get in trouble when he was done being consul. To get away, Caesar made sure he would be the next governor of Northern Italy and Southern France. This would also let him lead a lot of soldiers.

Chapter 3: Cleopatra as a Girl

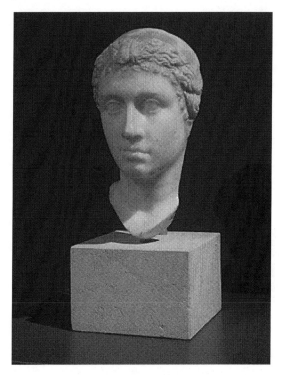

A statue bust of Cleopatra

Cleopatra was born over 2,000 years ago. People have talked about her since she was born. Men used to say that she was one of the most evil women to have ever lived. They said she tricked men into doing what she wanted them to do. Other people said that she was just a weak woman who kept falling in love with bad men.

Girls tell a different story about Cleopatra. They said that it was good that she was able to do so much. They said she set a good example for other women. She did this by getting just as much power for herself as men had. Some women even said that men listened to her because she was so smart.

Many people have talked about how she looked. Some people said that she was one of the prettiest women ever. But others say she wasn't pretty at all. A lot of artists have drawn pictures of her and made paintings of her. She looks different in their art.

Cleopatra was born in Alexandria, Egypt in 69 B.C. Her family had ruled Egypt for hundreds of years. She was related to Ptolemy. Ptolemy was one of Alexander the Great's generals. Ptolemy was Greek. That means Cleopatra was also Greek. Even though she was born in Egypt, she was not Egyptian.

Cleopatra's father had been the ruler of Egypt. The ruler was called pharaoh. Cleopatra's mother was also named Cleopatra. Her mother was called Cleopatra V because she was the 5th Cleopatra. Before she was well known, Cleopatra was only known as Cleopatra VII because she was the 7th Cleopatra. Now that everybody knows her, she's only called Cleopatra.

The family Cleopatra grew up in was not very good for a child. People were always trying to trick each other. Sometimes they even killed people who made them mad. Other people wanted to rule Egypt. One of the meanest men of was Cleopatra's own father. He was always afraid that someone was going to try to take over his country. He would not trust anyone else to help him rule Egypt. This was very hard on the people of Egypt. Many of them lived far away from Alexandria. That meant that they didn't know what was going on all the time. They often got mad. Sometimes they would even try to start wars against Cleopatra's father.

When Cleopatra was still a little girl, her father took her with him to Rome. Rome was very strong at the time. They wanted to take over Egypt too. They were stronger than Egypt so Cleopatra's father had to be nice to the Romans. Cleopatra and her father were in Rome for three years. While they were gone, Cleopatra's mother tried to take over the country. But her mother died just a few months after becoming queen. Many people think Cleopatra's older sister Berenice killed her. Berenice became queen after Cleopatra's mother.

Cleopatra's father did not like this. When he came back three years later, he brought a Roman army with him. When Berenice heard about this, she said she did not want to be queen anymore. She gave the power back to her father. Cleopatra's father was happy to be king again. But he was not happy that the Roman army was now a part of his country. For the rest of his life, he would need Rome's help to stay king.

While they were in Rome, Cleopatra and her father became very close. When she turned 14, he made her his regent. That meant that he had picked her to be queen after he died. He died 4 years later. Cleopatra was only 18 years old. A lot of Roman soldiers were in Egypt when she became queen.

Cleopatra had to deal with her younger brother too. Her 10 year old brother got to be king with her. She also had to marry him, even though they didn't like each other. People in Egypt also kept fighting against each other. Cleopatra's army had to fight them.

Egypt has a big river called the Nile River. The Nile River floods a lot. It usually floods every year. The Egyptians want it to flood because it helps them farm and grow food. But when

Cleopatra became queen, the Nile didn't flood enough. This meant Egypt had less food. Egypt also had to give Rome some of their food.

Cleopatra didn't want her brother to be king. But he had a lot of helpers with him. They thought he should be king because they didn't want a woman to rule Egypt. Cleopatra was also worried about the Romans. The Roman soldiers didn't leave Egypt. They wanted more power too.

Some Roman soldiers killed the sons of a famous Roman from Syria. Syria was Egypt's neighbor. Cleopatra had the men who killed these sons sent back to Rome. This made the other Roman soldiers mad. They hated Cleopatra. Two years later, they made her stop being queen. They let her brother be king all by himself.

An old statue bust of Cleopatra

Chapter 4: Caesar's Wars

Lyonel Royer's painting of a Gaul surrendering to Caesar

"I have fought sixty battles and I have learned nothing which I did not know at the beginning. Look at Caesar; he fought the first like the last." – Napoleon Bonaparte

In the first 40 years of his life, Caesar hadn't fought much. He had spent a lot of money though. He owed so much that Crassus couldn't even help him pay it all. Roman governors made a lot of money. That's why Caesar wanted to be a governor.

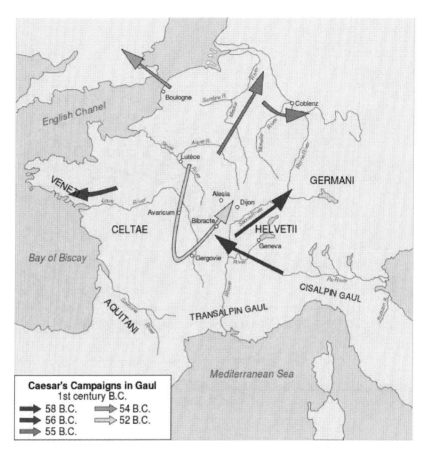

Caesar's Campaigns in Gaul
1st century B.C.
- 58 B.C.
- 56 B.C.
- 55 B.C.
- 54 B.C.
- 52 B.C.

The arrows are the different places Caesar fought from 58-52 B.C.

Roman governors made money by attacking other countries and taking their stuff. Caesar attacked some people in Germany first. When Caesar beat them, other people in the area started to fight him. Caesar attacked them in Belgium. But he was trapped near a river in 57 B.C. The fighting was going so badly that Caesar had to fight too. When his soldiers saw him fighting, they fought better. Caesar was able to win the battle.

After Caesar took control of Belgium, he fought in Gaul. Gaul was the name for France back then. In 55 B.C., Caesar beat more enemies in Germany. Then he led the first Romans into England.

In 54 B.C., Caesar had to fight in Gaul again. After he beat more enemies there, he took soldiers to England again. The Romans made a new town in England. They called it Londinium. Today it's called London. It's one of the biggest cities in the world.

Caesar wanted to keep being governor. But he was getting more powerful. Pompey didn't like this. He was jealous of Caesar. Pompey had married Caesar's daughter Julia. This would help make sure they didn't fight. But Julia died when Caesar was governor. Crassus also died in battle in 53 B.C. This meant Pompey and Caesar were the two strongest men in Rome.

Caesar wanted to go back to Rome. But in 52 B.C., the people in Gaul started fighting the Romans again. Caesar had to beat them one more time. Caesar's battles in Gaul are famous. This is because he wrote about them himself. Caesar's stories made people in Rome like him. His book is still used to teach Latin.

Chapter 5: Caesar Meets Cleopatra

In 50 B.C., Caesar was no longer governor and Pompey wanted to rule Rome. Pompey had a lot of friends in the Senate. The Senate told Caesar to come back to Rome. Caesar didn't want to come back though. He knew he would have to pay the money he owed. The Senate may even put him in jail. Caesar stayed near France instead.

The Senate called Caesar an enemy of Rome. Caesar knew he could only go to Rome if he had an army. In January of 49 B.C., Caesar and his army marched across the Rubicon River into Italy. That meant he was going to have to attack Pompey. He would have to attack Rome itself.

As Caesar and his army came to Rome, the Senate wanted Pompey to defend Rome. Pompey didn't think he had enough soldiers. Pompey left the city and didn't fight. Caesar took control of Rome. He was named Dictator by the Senators who were in Rome. A lot of Senators had left with Pompey.

Caesar hadn't won yet. He left his friend Mark Antony in charge of Rome. Caesar and his army went north and beat some of Pompey's soldiers in Spain. Then Caesar and his army went south to chase Pompey. Pompey sailed to Greece to get away.

M. Antonius.

A statue of Mark Antony

Pompey and Caesar fought in Greece. The battle was called the Battle of Dyrrachium. It was fought in July of 48 B.C. Pompey's army won, but Pompey didn't know it. When Caesar's army ran away, Pompey didn't have his men chase it. He thought Caesar was trying to trap him. Caesar said, "Victory today would have been the enemy's, if only anyone among them had possessed the good sense to grasp it".

The next time the armies fought, Caesar won. Pompey had lost the war. Caesar went back to Rome. He was named Dictator again. Pompey ran away to Egypt. Caesar heard that Pompey was trying to make a new army there. Caesar sailed to Egypt to stop him.

When Caesar got to Egypt, he found out Pompey was dead. Egypt's ruler had Pompey killed. He hoped this would make Caesar happy. But it made Caesar mad. He didn't think a Roman should be treated like that.

Cleopatra was the Egyptian king's sister. She wanted to rule Egypt herself. Caesar was staying in a palace. But Cleopatra couldn't let her brother's men see her. Then she had a great idea. She told her men to roll her up inside a rug and bring it to Caesar as a gift. When they brought

Caesar the rug, Cleopatra came out of it. They started talking. Caesar thought she was very pretty and soon fell in love with her. He also wanted her to be queen of Egypt.

A bust of Cleopatra

Cleopatra's brother did not like this. He ran away to get more men for his army. The soldiers came to Caesar's place and wouldn't let Caesar or Cleopatra leave. But Caesar also had Roman soldiers too. In January of 47 B.C., Caesar asked some friends to come help him and Cleopatra. 16,000 Roman soldiers came to Egypt. Cleopatra's brother had to run away from Alexandria. The Romans were better soldiers than the ones Cleopatra's brother had. In a battle, the Romans won. Cleopatra's brother died in the battle. This made Cleopatra the only ruler of Egypt.

Caesar was in Egypt for another three months. While he was there, Cleopatra gave birth to a boy. She named her son Caesarion. Many people thought he was Caesar's son. So did Cleopatra. But Caesar always said it was not his son. It would have made the Romans mad if he was.

After he won in Egypt, Caesar fought another war against Pontus. Then he heard that Cato the Younger wanted to fight him. Cato the Younger was liked by a lot of Romans. They thought he was a good man. He didn't like Caesar. He had run away from Rome when Caesar came back. Caesar's army beat Cato's army. Cato killed himself instead of letting Caesar take him prisoner.

A statue of Cato the Younger

After he beat Cato, Caesar was made Dictator in Rome. He was the only Consul too. This meant he could leave Rome again. He took an army to Spain and attacked some of Pompey's sons. He beat them in 45 B.C. When he came back to Rome, he was made Dictator for Life.

The Senate planned parties for Caesar after he won. But a lot of Romans were unhappy. They didn't like that Caesar was fighting other Romans. They were also mad that Caesar gave a lot of land to his soldiers. Some Senators who didn't like him saw that people were mad. They started making plans against Caesar.

In 46 and 45 B.C., Caesar made new laws in Rome. He also said that his nephew Octavian would be his heir.

A statue of Octavian made around 30 B.C.

Caesar also had a new calendar made. It was called the Julian calendar. It is the same calendar we use today! The month of July was named after Julius Caesar himself!

Chapter 6: The Ides of March

"I have lived long enough both in years and in accomplishments." - Caesar

Caesar knew he had enemies. But he did not know how mad some people were. Some Senators were very mad when Caesar had coins made in his honor. Coins were usually only made for dead Romans. And when he was talking in Rome one time, a friend of his put a laurel wreath on a statue of him. That was only done for gods and kings. This made many Romans mad.

Caesar tried to tell Romans that he wasn't king. When one crowd cheered him by shouting "king, king, king" at him, he made them stop. When Mark Antony tried to give him a laurel wreath, Caesar wouldn't let him. But people still knew Caesar had all the power. In 45 B.C., 60 men began to make plans. They called themselves the Liberators. They wanted to kill Caesar. They were led by a Senator named Marcus Brutus. Brutus had been good friends with Caesar. Caesar loved him so much that he treated Brutus like a son.

Statue of Marcus Brutus

Brutus didn't like that Caesar had all the power. He wanted the Senate to still have power. He and his friends planned to kill Caesar in the Senate.

On the morning of March 15, 44 B.C., Caesar's wife asked him not to go to the Senate. March 15 was known as the Ides of March. Caesar's wife had heard that men were planning to kill him. Caesar was going to stay home. But then Brutus came to Caesar's house. He told Caesar it wouldn't look good if the Dictator of Rome wouldn't come to the Senate. This changed Caesar's mind. Caesar then left for the Senate as he had planned.

Mark Antony had also heard about people planning to kill Caesar. One of the men in the plan was named Servilius Casca. Casca didn't want to kill Caesar. He told Antony about the plan. Antony tried to stop Caesar at the steps of the Senate. But some of the other people in the plan found Antony. They moved him away from Caesar.

When Caesar went in the Senate, a man named Tillius Cimber came up to him. Cimber said he needed to talk to Caesar about his brother. When Caesar tried to walk past him, Cimber grabbed Caesar's clothes. When Cimber grabbed him, Caesar said, "What is this violence?"

Casca had told Antony about the plot. But now he decided to attack Caesar. He walked up to

Caesar. Then he pulled out a knife and tried to stab Caesar in the neck. He didn't hurt Caesar very badly though. Caesar grabbed him by the neck and said, "What are you doing, you wretch?" Casca got scared and drop his knife. Then he said, "Help me, brothers!" The other men in the plot then ran at Caesar. There were almost 60 of them.

The Senators were not soldiers. They didn't know how to use a knife very well. But there were too many of them for Caesar. Caesar was stabbed again and again by the men. He tripped and fell to the ground. The men kept stabbing him while he was on the ground. Caesar was stabbed almost 25 times. Even though they stabbed him a lot, doctors who saw his body said only one of the stabbings was bad enough to kill him.

Jean-Léon Gérôme's painting of Caesar's death

Karl Von Piloty's painting. It's called *The Assassination of Caesar*

Vincenzo Camuccini's painting. It's called *Death of Julius Caesar*

The plan worked. Julius Caesar was dead. The Senators hoped that this would let the Senate take power. But a lot of Romans had liked Caesar. His friend Mark Antony and his nephew Octavian fought the people who had killed Caesar. Then Antony and Octavian fought each other. When Octavian won, he became the emperor of Rome. He called himself Caesar Augustus.

Julius Caesar once said, "I love the name of honor, more than I fear death." He got his wish. Caesar is the most famous Roman. He is also one of the most famous men in history. Everyone thinks he was one of the best military leaders ever. Because of Caesar, Rome was ruled by emperors for 500 years. The emperors called themselves Caesars. Kings in other countries used his name too. In Russia, the king called himself Czar. In Germany, the ruler called himself Kaiser. These names came from Julius Caesar's name.

Chapter 7: Cleopatra and Mark Antony

After Caesar died, Cleopatra was worried about her son. She was afraid he could not ever be king of Egypt because people thought his father was a Roman. So she had to make another plan for his future. First, she had her own brother killed. Then she made her son her regent. This meant that she would share power with him.

Cleopatra also watched what was going on in Rome. The Romans were fighting each other again. Cleopatra wanted to help one side. That way, the side she picked would help Egypt if they won. Cleopatra decided to have Egypt help Mark Antony. He was Julius Caesar's friend. He had started a war against the men who killed Caesar.

A statue of Mark Antony

The Romans who were fighting against Mark Antony were named Cassius and Marcus Brutus. They were mad when Cleopatra picked Antony. They wanted to attack Egypt and make sure she wasn't queen anymore. But then they had to go back to Rome. Cleopatra was safe.

A statue of Marcus Brutus

Cassius and Brutus left one of their friends and their navy near Egypt. When Cleopatra's ships started sailing to where Mark Antony was, they wanted to attack Cleopatra's ships. But then there was a big storm. It sank many of the Egyptian ships. It also made Cleopatra very sick. She had to go back to Egypt.

Cleopatra was sick for weeks. But then she heard Mark Antony had beaten the other army. He and two other people were now the rulers of Rome. Their names were Octavian and Lepidus. Antony was in charge of the eastern part of the Roman Empire.

In 41 B.C., Antony sent a letter to Cleopatra. He told her to come to Rome because he wanted to talk to her. He had heard that she liked his side better. But he also heard that she gave money to Cassius so he wouldn't attack Egypt. Antony wanted to find out what really happened. He also wanted to find out if she would help him with a new war he was in.

Cleopatra met Mark Antony during the winter of 41 BC. Like Caesar, Antony fell in love with her. When he stayed with her all winter instead of going home to his family, people were mad. They got even madder when he helped Cleopatra kill her sister.

A painting of Antony and Cleopatra

In 40 B.C., Antony stopped talking to Cleopatra. He may have been afraid of what other Romans were saying. He may have felt bad because he had a wife already. Antony went back to Rome. But on his way to Rome, he heard his wife had died. Antony married Octavian's sister. This would help make sure Octavian and Antony didn't fight each other. A few months after Antony left, Cleopatra gave birth to twins. Their names were Alexander and Cleopatra. They were Mark Antony's children.

After Cleopatra had twins, Antony's part of the Roman Empire was attacked. He had his friends help him make an army. But as he was going to battle, he stopped in Greece. He started calling himself the Greek god Dionysus. Dionysus was the god of wine. Antony did this because he liked to drink a lot of wine.

When Antony was in Greece, the Roman army left. They wouldn't help him. This made him very mad. He decided to leave his wife and children. He went to Alexandria to be with Cleopatra. Cleopatra was going to give him money to fight his new war. Cleopatra also married Antony.

After Antony married Cleopatra, he went to his new war. Things went well for him at first. But then he lost a lot of men. They were getting sick and leaving his army. He had to go back to Egypt. He didn't win the war. The Egyptians thought the gods didn't like Antony. They thought he lost because he had left his wife and children in Rome.

Antony and Cleopatra didn't seem to care what was happening in Rome. Antony just wanted to stay in Egypt with Cleopatra. He liked how people lived in Egypt. When Antony fought another war in 34 B.C., he was trying to help Egypt get more land. He wasn't even fighting for Rome anymore.

Antony won that war, so Cleopatra wanted to have a big party. Her party was like a Roman party. During the party, Antony and Cleopatra's three children were given royal titles. Cleopatra was named Queen of Queens and ruler of the East. Her son, Caesarion, was named King of Kings, ruler of Egypt and the East, living God, and above all. Antony also said that he was no longer friends with the men he had known back in Rome. He said Egypt was free of Rome. This was not a good thing for Cleopatra and Antony to do.

An old coin with Cleopatra's face

Chapter 8: The Last War

In 33 and 32 B.C., Rome and Egypt were getting ready to fight each other. In Egypt, Antony and Cleopatra said Julius Caesar's nephew Octavian should not rule Rome. They said that Cleopatra's son Caesarion should rule Rome. This was because they said Caesarion was Julius Caesar's real son. They also said he would be a better ruler.

This was not a good thing to say to Octavian. The main reason that people liked him was because they had liked Caesar. Antony had also divorced Octavian's sister. He and Cleopatra also said that they might stop sending food to Rome.

A statue of Octavian made around 30 B.C.

Octavian was mad at Antony for going to war without asking him. He said Antony was not a real Roman. He made Romans mad at Antony. He told them Antony was living like a king in Egypt while the Romans didn't.

In 32 B.C., Octavian told Rome that he was going to war against Cleopatra. He did not say he was going to war against Antony. He didn't want it to seem like he was fighting a Roman. This would make some Romans mad. But a lot of Romans picked Cleopatra's side. They wanted to help Antony. They made a big army. They even talked about attacking the city of Rome itself.

In 31 B.C., Octavian had an army. He sailed to Greece with his ships and soldiers. A lot of the Romans who were in Cleopatra's army wanted to fight for Octavian. Many of them had fought for Julius Caesar. They didn't want to fight against Caesar's nephew. Cleopatra and Antony had to go back to Egypt. They made a lot of ships and got their own army.

On September 2, 31 B.C., Antony and Cleopatra were in a bad place. Their boats were trapped by Octavian's boats. Cleopatra told Antony to attack Octavian's ships so they could try to get away. But Cleopatra and Antony knew they would probably lose. The big sea battle was called the Battle of Actium.

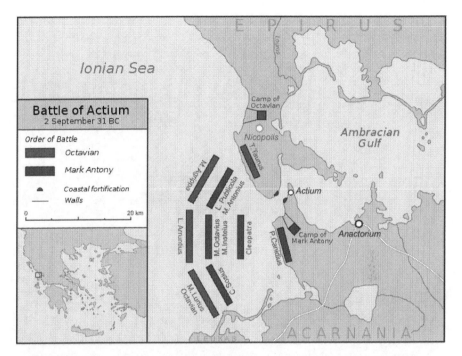

The Battle of Actium. The purple line is Cleopatra and Antony's ships. The red line is Octavian's ships.

Antony and Cleopatra had 500 ships. 250 of those ships were very big. They had five decks and were big enough that if they ran into Octavian's ships, they could sink Octavian's ships. Octavian had only 250 ships. They were much smaller than Antony's. But this meant they could sail faster than Antony's ships.

During the battle, the water had a lot of waves. This helped Octavian's ships because they were easier to sail. They were less affected by the waves. Antony and Cleopatra also had a lot of sick sailors. They couldn't fight. This meant that a lot of Antony's ships didn't have enough sailors. His big ships couldn't run into Octavian's ships if they didn't have enough men to row them.

Octavian's smaller ships were able to sail around Antony's ships. They shot Antony's men with fire arrows. Some of Octavian's sailors jumped on Antony's ships and started fighting sailors on their own ship. And Octavian's smaller ships could run away before the big ships hit them.

After a few hours, Antony and Cleopatra knew they were losing. More and more of their ships were being sunk. Some of their ships were burning too. Cleopatra and Antony had their own ships behind their navy. Cleopatra and Antony had their ships sail away from the battle and go back to Egypt. They left the rest of their boats to lose to Octavian.

A painting of the Battle of Actium

The Battle of Actium was a very big battle. It meant that Octavian would be the ruler of Rome. It was very bad for Cleopatra and Antony. But Antony thought he could still beat Octavian. He had more than 10,000 men on horses. He also had a lot of soldiers. But when he lost the Battle of Actium, a lot of his soldiers left him and joined Octavian's side.

Antony was very mad that his army left. He yelled at Cleopatra. He thought Cleopatra was helping Octavian to save her own life. Cleopatra was so afraid that she locked herself in a room. She wouldn't let Antony in. She had a helper take a note to Antony. The note said that Cleopatra had killed herself.

The note was not true. Cleopatra had not killed herself. But Antony thought she was dead. He didn't want to live if she was dead. Antony took out his sword and stabbed himself. When he cried and yelled, Cleopatra heard him. She found out Antony had killed himself.

Cleopatra may have wanted to trick Antony into killing himself. This would let her talk to Octavian. But when she saw Antony die, she got mad at herself. She tore her clothes off her body. She started trying to pull out her own hair. She was still mad at herself when Octavian's soldiers showed up. They made Cleopatra a prisoner.

Cleopatra knew that she would be treated badly by Octavian. She didn't want to go back to Rome. She decided to kill herself. People still talk about how she killed herself. Nobody is sure how she did it. Most people think she had a snake bite her. Egypt had a lot of snakes with poison. She may have even kept one as a pet. A lot of people think she let a snake called an asp bite her. But it may have been a cobra. Some people think there was no snake at all. They think Cleopatra drank hemlock. Hemlock was a poison. Other people think Octavian had her killed.

A statue of a snake biting Cleopatra

When Cleopatra died, Octavian was the ruler of Egypt. He had Cleopatra's sons put to death. Cleopatra's family had ruled Egypt for 300 years. But Cleopatra would be the last ruler in her family.

Cleopatra didn't do everything right. She made some bad choices. But people still think of her as a great woman today. People like that Cleopatra tried to be a powerful woman. They also like to study her life. A lot of things about Cleopatra are still not known. People are still trying to figure it all out.

Cleopatra died over 2,000 years ago. But she is still the best known woman in history!

49075618R00022

Made in the USA
Columbia, SC
15 January 2019